IN A JAPANESE GARDEN

Charmaine Aserappa
Original Woodcuts by Akiko Naomura

Council Oak Books
San Francisco / Tulsa

One night,
I wished for
a Japanese garden, tranquil and serene;
but I lived in an apartment, walled in by the city.

The next morning, I awoke to ripples of light, dancing across the room.

I looked out my window. It had rained during the night. The flat roof of the garage outside had turned into a perfect reflecting pool.

Autumn leaves floated on the surface. An old plank propped against the red brick wall made a wooden bridge. The copper cover of the ventilator shaft curved like the roof of a temple. Sparrows sipped at the edge of the pool.

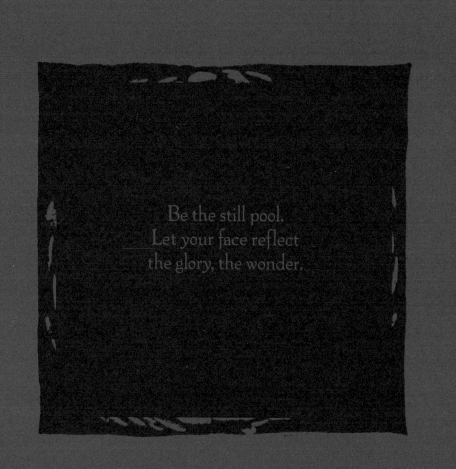

Be the still pool.
Let your face reflect
the glory, the wonder.

Be the dragonfly,
silent but joyful.

Be the bud.
Prepare to blossom.

Be the tree.
Grant shelter.

Be the butterfly.
Accept the riches of the moment.

Be the moth.
Seek the light.

Be the lantern.
Guide the lost.

Be the path.
—   Open the way for another.

Be the wind chime.
Let the breeze blow through you.
Turn the storms into song.

Be the rain.
Wash away, cleanse,
forgive.

Be the grass.
Grow back when you
are trod upon.

Be the bridge.
Reach in peace
toward the other side.

Be the soil.
Bear fruit.

Be the moss.
Temper your strength
with softness,
with mercy.

Be the gardener.
Create order.

Be the temple.
Let the Spirit dwell in you.

Be the seasons.
Welcome change.

Be the moon.
Shine through the darkness.

Trust in the circle.
To end is to begin.

Be the pebble.
Let time shape and smooth you.

Be the leaf.
Fall gracefully when your time comes
to let go.

JAPANESE GARDENS are not merely decorative, but are meticulously designed and maintained as meditative spaces for contemplation, refreshment and reflection. Traditional elements are carefully placed to represent different aspects of the universe.

The simple images and spare words in this little book resonate so deeply because these traditional Buddhist elements yield symbolic meaning across spiritual traditions. A few interpretations are given here, to enrich one's experience of a real—or imaginary—garden; each person will ultimately find his or her own meaning.

POOL: A pool is placed in a Japanese garden to unite the reflection of the sky with the earth, symbolizing the wholeness of the universe. In Western tradition, the pool evokes healing baptismal waters, which wash away sin and bring rebirth.

TREE: In a Japanese garden, trees are pruned to exert the discipline of art over nature, revealing the intrinsic shape of the tree and symbolizing the shaping of character and the shedding of bad habits and worldly distractions. Christian and Judaic traditions see the trees of life and knowledge.

LANTERN: Often placed by a tea house in a Japanese garden, the lantern symbolically illuminates the path through life. Christian symbology pictures Jesus holding a lantern as the light of the world, seeking lost souls to save.

WIND CHIME: A dimension of sound is added to the garden as the wind blows through the leaves or chimes. Wind, along with earth, fire, sky, and water, is considered to be one of the five elements of nature. The wind gathers the words from Tibetan prayer flags and sends them heavenward. It also symbolizes the animating breath of life, and the holy spirit of Christian belief.

ROCK: Rocks are carefully placed in a Japanese garden to symbolize stability and long life. In dry landscape gardens, gravel is often raked into precise patterns around a rock, symbolic of the currents of the sea flowing around an island. Christian tradition sees the church as the rock, solid and eternal. Jews place small rocks atop gravestones, in remembrance.

CIRCLE: The circle represents the rebirth of nature, the cycle of cause and effect, the smooth flow of life energy, and the perpetual unfolding of a divine plan in which each living creature plays a unique part.

ACKNOWLEDGMENTS

I deeply appreciate the people who helped to make *In a Japanese Garden*:
my mother; Gladys May Aserappa; my son, Nicolas Bernard Re;
and countless friends, colleagues, and family members too numerous to
mention here. I am very grateful to you all.
Special thanks to Jennifer Barrows,
a light to the homeless.
C. A.

Council Oak Books, LLC, 2822 Van Ness Avenue
San Francisco CA 94109;
1350 E. 15th Street, Tulsa, OK 74120

First Edition / First Printing.

Printed in South Korea.
ISBN 1-57178-086-6

Book and jacket design by Renée N. Khatami.

05 04 03 02 01 99   5 4 3 2 1

Charmaine Aserappa is a community worker and mother in Brooklyn, New York, with a background in fine book publishing. Born in India to an English mother and a Sri Lankan father, Charmaine was exposed to a wide variety of religions and remains a Christian. A percentage of her proceeds from the book will be donated to environmental conservation.

Akiko Naomura, a human service worker in New York City, comes from Fukuoka City, Japan. Her fine-art lithographs of her Greenwich Village neighborhood have recently been exhibited in Japan. Akiko handmade the woodcuts for *In a Japanese Garden* by a traditional method, carving the images into blocks of pine, which were inked and printed onto rice paper. Akiko is a Buddhist.